Every Day with Jesus

TREASURY

SELWYN HUGHES

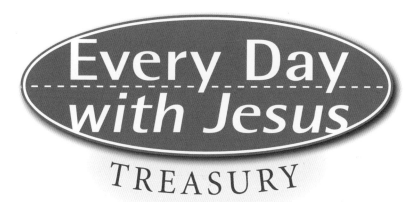

TREASURY

Dedicated to the great army of *Every Day with Jesus* readers across the world whose constant encouragement and letters of appreciation have helped me continue in times when I might easily have given up.

Contents

Preface

In 1965 a small group of people asked my help in guiding them in their daily devotions. Little did I realise when I first responded to them that my writing would develop through various stages to where it is today. First, my thoughts were put down on handwritten postcards that covered a theme for one week. Then, as other people discovered them, I had to resort to printed cards. Soon the writing developed into a theme for one month and eventually it took the form it is today – a devotional that covers a single theme over a period of two months.

The book you now hold in your hands contains some highlights from a few of the favourite issues over the years. These issues have been chosen because of the number of letters we received from people in response to them, saying how God had used *Every Day with Jesus* to reach into their lives and draw them closer to Himself. My wish is that through this book God will do the same for you.

We estimate that including the current bimonthly issues and the various *Every Day with Jesus* publications, such as the one-year editions, close on a million people read these devotions daily. I can't tell how grateful I am to God for His help and guidance in the choice of themes and His continued blessing upon the publication.

To Him be all the glory

Selwyn Hughes
Waverley Abbey House, Farnham, Surrey

Foreword

Arriving home from our family vacation in 1977, I was amazed to find an envelope in my Southern California mailbox from CWR in England requesting permission to publish my poems. The letter explained that a man named Selwyn Hughes had seen a collection of my poems in a US magazine and wanted to use several of them in his CWR worldwide Prayer Diary for 1978. Who were these far-away people, I wondered, and why would they pluck a fledgling writer like me to be involved in this amazing project?

But I was pleased to allow them to use my writing, and thus began decades of delight in working with these dear servants of God. Very soon my poems began to spill over onto the inside front cover of Selwyn's wonderful *Every Day with Jesus* devotional guide where they have continued for over 27 years.

In the early years of working together I discovered how beautifully God's Spirit bridges continents to unite hearts. Although we had never met in person, I felt close to Selwyn and so many other dear ones at CWR. And I was touched by and drawn close to the precious readers who began writing to me from all over the world. Eventually God brought me to the UK, and how wonderful that was as my husband and I celebrated our 25th wedding anniversary with our CWR friends. Later, I visited twice more to speak at the beautiful Waverley Abbey House and in London.

On one of those visits, Selwyn asked if I would be interested in writing poems to specifically match his *EDWJ* subjects. I was. Selwyn is an inspired writer, full of wisdom and understanding, so it has been quite a challenge seeking to capture his rich themes in just a few lines for each issue. But I've been honoured to try, and so very blessed to share these pages with Selwyn for close to three decades.

Susan Lenzkes
January 2005

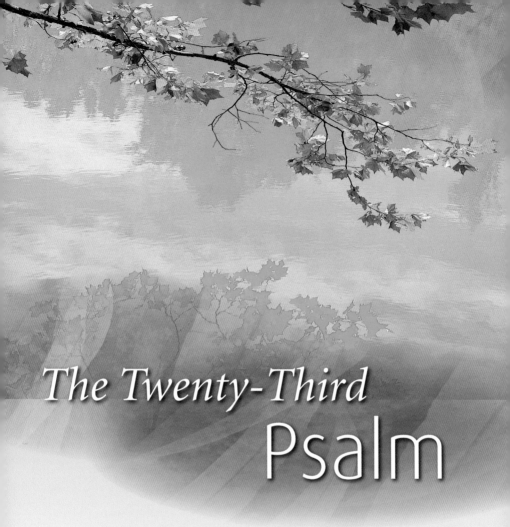

The Twenty-Third
Psalm

'He tends his flock like a shepherd: He
gathers the lambs in his arms and carries
them close to his heart; he gently leads
those that have young.'
ISAIAH 40:11

Quiet Time

I know some,
a few,
whose lives are a bold
exclamation point!
They drive hard in a slashing
downstroke
toward a distant goal
no larger than a
dot.
Yet somehow they never connect.
And I know some,
too many,
whose searching lives
are a question mark.
I find them wandering,
curving and sloping
toward that elusive dot of
answer.
They, too, never reach the goal.
But there are others,
too few,
whose lives are a
simple statement.
They do not reach for the truth –
they live in it.
They know Jesus.
Period.

Taken from *When the Handwriting on the Wall is in Brown Crayon*
by Susan Lenzkes. Copyright © 2000 by Susan Lenzkes and used by
permission of Discovery House Publishers, Box 3566, Grand Rapids
MI 49501. All rights reserved.

EVERY REFRESHMENT AND COMFORT WE NEED FOR life's difficult experiences are held in this psalm. Straightaway, 'The LORD is my Shepherd', brings us to our heart relationship with God, to look at how well we *really* know Him, using imagery of tender care, bringing us a truthful picture of our loving God.

Our God provides

'I shall not be in want': disaster may surround us, but we never lack the 'expert care and tender supervision' of our Shepherd helping turn our 'stumbling-blocks into stepping stones'. In 1 Peter 5 we read: 'Cast all your anxiety on him because he cares for you' (v.7). Our perspective altered, we know God won't allow any situation where 'He cannot work for our good and for His own eternal glory'.

Christ's presence spells freedom, enabling us to 'lie down in green pastures', free from fear, attack and hunger: 'There is no fear in love. But perfect love drives out fear' (1 John 4:18). Focus on Christ and receive His peace, sure that He will discipline where needed, pour out His divine grace when the enemy attacks, and feed us with His Word. Allow the Shepherd to lead you 'beside quiet waters', and the Word's life-giving strength is yours.

'He restores my soul': the 'tenderness, the compassion and the patience' Jesus showed Peter after he had denied Him is ours, even rescuing us when we stray into danger, for God desires our deliverance and restoration. The Lord can 'restore you to health and heal your wounds' (Jer. 30:17), replacing your weariness with enthusiasm.

Keeping close to our God of all comfort

God also leads us 'in paths of righteousness for his name's sake'. But, even knowing our stubbornness will take us into danger, He won't force us on the right way, allowing us to realise that, unless we follow *the* Way, self-destruction follows. Our alternative is to take up our cross, and put our lives into Christ's hands, just as He put His life into His Father's hands. Then we are led from 'one good pasture to another', receiving 'fresh revelation' from His Word.

Even though we 'walk through the valley of the shadow of death' the Lord remains close: 'I will fear no evil, for you are with me'. As Christians, we walk with the Lord 'into an eternity of endless delight'. Grace will bring us through physical death to the 'dwelling place' that Christ promises us, free of judgment as we give our lives to Him – free of death because of the cross.

'Your rod and your staff, they comfort me': just as a shepherd uses the rod and staff to protect and discipline his sheep, so God disciplines and comforts us, because 'He has the deepest concern … for our spiritual development and wellbeing'. It is His love, not our fear, that keeps us from danger and draws us close to Him. David recognises, too, that the Shepherd goes ahead to ensure safe grazing for His flock: 'You prepare a table before me in the presence of my enemies'. Closeness to God guarantees our safety and, each time we remember our deliverance, our confidence in Him grows. We must remember, too, the price Christ paid to bring us into absolute 'contentment and security': His life.

Our God delivers, restores and assures

'You anoint my head with oil; my cup overflows': we ask and Jesus will minister 'the soothing oil of the Spirit' to our hurts, and when we are surrounded by 'life's irritations', He brings relief. When the enemy tries to pull us away from our Saviour, focusing on Him brings us back into safety. Paul tells us: 'If anything is excellent or praiseworthy – think about such things' (Phil. 4:8). Turn to the Lord, ask for help – *and He will deliver.*

God also restores, following 'hard on our heels to redeem every ... situation' – as David exclaims: 'Surely goodness and love will follow me all the days of my life'. The Lord brings good even out of situations caused by sin, carelessness or ignorance; when we look back our lives bear the Redeemer's mark, so we may learn by our mistakes. Unshakeable faith in our faithful God transforms everything, knowing the last word is with Him.

Then God pours His reassurance into us, so that David could say: 'I will dwell in the house of the LORD for ever'. David was confident of his life in eternity. Remember that assurance is yours once you surrender your life to Christ: 'I tell you the truth, he who believes has everlasting life' (John 6:47). How we long to be 'at home' with the Shepherd!

Every Day with Jesus
July/August 1985

Quotes

Knowing the psalm is one
thing – hearsay – but knowing
the Shepherd is quite another
– heartsay.

*Coolness in place of heat, and peace instead of torment are the
rewards of those who are swift to turn to the Shepherd and invite
Him to minister to them in this way. So when thoughts seem to
niggle you and almost drive you up the wall, draw close to the
Shepherd and let Him apply the oil of the Spirit to your troubled
and anxious mind. And you need have no fears that His supply
of oil is limited in any way. He draws from a cup that never runs
dry: 'Thou anointest my head with oil, my cup overflows'.*

... whenever I am beset by troubles and
trials the thing that quietens and reassures
my spirit is the keen awareness that my
Shepherd is nearby. There is nothing like
Christ's presence to dispel the tension, the
panic and the terror of the unknown.

Quotes

... it is God's desire to daily lead His sheep to the 'still waters' of Scripture so that He might slake their spiritual thirst and prepare them for the day ahead.

God follows hard on the heels of every event and circumstance in our lives, not only teaching us a great deal, but working to turn every loss into a gain. Look back over your life for a moment. Have there not been times when you questioned God's wisdom and management of your affairs? Have you not had moments when you thought you could survive better on your own? But what is your view now? Are you not convinced that He followed you in goodness and mercy? Did not good come out of the evil, light out of darkness, and faith out of despair?

Reflection

The picture of Christ as a Shepherd, carefully leading and taking a personal interest in His sheep has been a great comfort to men and women through the ages. We must be careful how we interpret the terms, 'leading and taking a personal interest in His sheep' however. Some believe it to mean that God will never allow bad things to happen to His children. Thus they become disappointed when tragedies strike them and think God has abandoned them. God's shepherding of His children means that He will only allow into our lives those things that He can transform into good (see Rom. 8:28–29). If God can see no good can be brought out of something that is coming our way, He will intervene to stop it. As our Shepherd He forestalls some things, allows others when He sees they can be turned to good, and in it all never leaves us or forsakes us.

Prayer

Gracious and loving Shepherd, forgive me if I have interpreted your shepherding of my life to mean I will never have to face any troubles. Help me take comfort in the fact that no matter what happens, You will never leave my side. Thank You my Father. Amen.

The Divine
Eagle

'... but those who hope in the LORD will renew
their strength. They will soar on wings like
eagles; they will run and not grow weary,
they will walk and not be faint.'
ISAIAH 40:31

Quiet Time

I lay at your feet, God,
prostrate with the knowledge of
who I am
and
WHO YOU ARE.
As Your mighty hand descends,
my understanding trembles in dread
of its awesome weight!
But so softly it comes,
hovering
like protective wings
over my fragile dependency.
I do not know the heel of Your hand.
You do not press or crush
but touch my spirit with
gentle fingers –
a hand caressing.
Then tenderly You
lift my humility to meet the
love
nailed in the palm of Your
mighty hand.

Susan Lenzkes, copyright © 1981

IKE THE MOTHER EAGLE, WHO STIRS UP HER EAGLETS'
nest and pushes them out to fly, God doesn't want us to stay as
we are! God uses our discomforts and disappointments, upsetting
us 'in order to set us up'. Persecution scattered the Early Church, and
our Lord's going released the unlimited power of His presence in the
disciples as they received the Holy Spirit. James tells us: 'Consider it pure
joy … whenever you face trials of many kinds' (James 1:2). It is our
attitude that helps us 'soar on wings like eagles' (Isa. 40:31) into our
Father's presence.

Letting go – to let God take hold

Are we sure who *really* owns our possessions? God soon shakes us out of
any delusions because He 'wants our gaze fully focused on Himself', not
on things. Paul's statement that 'the love of money is a root of all kinds
of evil' (1 Tim. 6:10) underlines the importance of our relationship to
possessions.

Understanding the beauty of surrendering something we never owned,
we see that *everything* we do is part of God's calling – 'if it furthers the
kingdom' – as we make *His* money work. Once surrendered, we are 'then
free to cultivate generosity', which brings God's blessings, money under
Christ's control being 'purified and redeemed'.

We also rob ourselves of our true potential by snuggling down in our
nest of spiritual complacency. Jesus said: 'I have come that they may have
life, and have it to the full' (John 10:10). Do you have the 'energising
power of the Spirit' – indeed, does He have *you*? As Jesus reflects the
Father, so our Lord reflects the Holy Spirit and, by surrendering to the
Spirit, we become more Christlike. Jesus reveals the 'Spirit of power and
… purity', and *we can be like Him*. This can happen to us – empowered
and cleansed in our hearts like the disciples after Pentecost.

Soaring higher from a position of weakness

The Creator, God, makes us with a capacity for creative living, but only when completely 'dedicated to God' do we have 'the potential for a fully dynamic and adventurous life' – another reason why the Lord pushes us out of the nest. If we resist Him, we risk leaving our God-given destiny unfulfilled by staying in our 'rut'. He may give us an amazing thought or idea, which challenges us, and could transform us: allow Christ to 'break the stalemate' and stimulate your mind to be fit for the kingdom!

As the Divine Eagle pushes us out of the nest, He challenges us to remove our masks, desiring 'truth in the inner parts' (Psa. 51:6). As we let God have His way, He gently helps us accept ourselves, with all our hurts, for only by acknowledging our weaknesses can we start to grow 'toward the goal that He has set' for our lives. When we see ourselves as God sees us, we start to blossom, allowing God to bring us to our 'full maturity in Christ' (Col. 1:28, Phillips), changing us into His image. We can then help others in our weakness – but with His strength.

Sometimes God overturns our nest to shake and deepen our 'troubled' faith, making us examine what we *really* believe – and *who* we believe in – so that in uncertain times we can stand firm, fear-free. As 'all things were created by him and for him' (Col. 1:16), then 'science can never invalidate God. It only confirms Him'. Christ returned from the wilderness 'in the power of the Spirit', and was able to pass on a 'serene and joyous faith' to His disciples. Then there is enormous comfort – and verification of God's power – in the worldwide Body of Christ. Challenge helps 'troubled faith' become 'triumphant faith'.

No more games – just Christ-centred teamwork

Paul writes: 'When I became a man, I put childish ways behind me' (1 Cor. 13:11); another reason why God nudges us out of the nest is so we stop playing 'childish' games. Moses played the 'yes … but' game, so afraid of failure that he gave excuses for not obeying God – forgetting that God always equips. We can avoid spiritual intimacy with God, refuse to accept responsibility, run away from Him, or 'act stupid', like Peter did, when he denied the Lord: all reinforce our fears. Sometimes we expect God to do everything, not realising we can 'soar into the air and enjoy the freedom of being mature'!

Then there is the 'denominational nest', which can be a powerful barrier to our 'true unity in Christ' so beloved of the Lord. We read in John 17: 'that all of them may be one' (v.21). Throughout history God has used the Holy Spirit's ministry to stir up the churches so that we may see that He is 'bigger than a denomination'. He has also stirred up His people to distinguish between 'man-made traditions and unchanging truths of God'. Showing the world 'the unity of the Spirit through the bond of peace' (Eph. 4:3) in a Christ-centred fellowship, differences can be 'growing points' not causes for division, and His Church can 'truly become one'.

Every Day with Jesus
September/October 1981

Quotes

"God has designed us for creative living, creative thinking and creative venture."

Self-acceptance does not mean that we are content to remain as we are, but that we love ourselves with the same kind, considerate and patient love with which God loves us. When I see that my growth and advancement in the Christian life is not a condition for God loving me, that I do not have to improve in order to earn His love, then this takes the pressure to perform off my personality and I grow as do the lilies – effortlessly and without toil.

How should we treat such troubles when we find the nest of life's calm and comfortable experiences overturned? We should look upon them as an opportunity to expand our spiritual wings, soar to new heights in the heavenlies and make some fresh discoveries about ourselves and God, our heavenly Father.

Quotes

I saw my need in two terms – power and purity. I cried out for both. God graciously met me at the point of my need, filled me with such power that it transformed me from a shy, diffident teenager into a preacher of the gospel … My Pentecostal friends would say that in that crisis I received the baptism in the Spirit. My Holiness friends would say that my heart was sanctified by faith. All I know is that … God met my need for both power and purity. And, my dear friend, what He did for me, He can do for you.

This gripping truth of God pushing us forward into greater usefulness – the Divine Eagle throwing us out of the nest to make us fly – is a divine principle that is deeply embedded in Scripture.

Reflection

In David McNally's magnificent book *Even Eagles Need a Push*, he makes the point that until an eaglet discovers its wings there is no purpose for its life. Eagles are made to soar, they are built to fly. 'But the thrill of soaring,' says David McNally 'has to begin with a push' – the encouragement a mother eagle gives its young to get them out of the nest. A 'push' is the greatest gift a mother eagle can give its young. It is the same with the Almighty. If God did not push us toward the fulfilling of our potential then many of us would never leave our 'comfort zone' and thus remain stultified and undeveloped. Is God stirring up your nest at the moment? Does everything seem topsy-turvy in your life? Take heart, it could be that God is preparing you for the higher heights.

Prayer

My Father and my God, forgive me if I prefer the 'comfort zone' to the challenge of daring and doing for You. If I need a 'push' then help me be obedient to Your pure and perfect purposes. Help me see it also as a supreme act of love. In Jesus' name. Amen.

The Lord's
Prayer

'This, then, is how you should
pray: "Our Father in heaven,
hallowed be your name"'
MATTHEW 6:9

Quiet Time

Teach me, Lord!
I know I need to learn a lesson
of restraint
or priorities,
else I would never be this tired.
But teach me, Father,
not from the distance of heaven
nor from behind a pulpit
or podium,
but from within the
circle of Your Father-Arms.
Teach me Your tender love
as I rest on Your
Mighty Shoulder,
then whisper to me
what I keep forgetting –
I must rest within Your arms
constantly
if I am to rest within Your will.

Susan Lenzkes, copyright © 1983

'**O**UR FATHER IN HEAVEN, HALLOWED BE YOUR NAME …'
Simply yet profoundly 'the Master presents a model of praying
that touches on every major aspect of prayer' – whatever we
pray in line with it brings us close to the Father's heart. Each word
is precious. 'Our Father' reflects our intimacy as believing children
with our Creator; and we see the true, wonderfully positive, nature of
fatherhood in His Son, Jesus: 'Anyone who has seen me has seen the
Father' (John 14:9).

Our holy and loving Father

The prayer unfolds, as does our 'true perspective': focusing on God, we
see who He is – our loving Father – and where He is – 'in heaven'. When
our imagination's prime focus is gazing at the Father 'all the doors of the
personality fly open'. Jesus tells us to lift our 'spiritual vision' to God's
limitless kingdom, where He is 'high and exalted' (Isa. 6:1). In Psalm 19,
'The heavens declare the glory of God' (v.1) – all creation reflects Him,
who draws us to draw upon *His* endless spiritual resources.

'Hallowed be your name': amazingly we are to pray on God's behalf
first, acknowledging His holiness and superiority. Indeed, Jesus said, 'I
will do whatever you ask *in my name*, so that the Son may bring glory
to the Father' (John 14:13, my italics). 'When we honour God's name,
we honour Him', because His name stands for who He is. Recognising
His character we submit willingly to Him in reverence – before bringing
Him our requests, *in line with His character*. How wonderful – a holy
God, who allows us to call Him 'Daddy'!

How He wants us to pray

'But seek first his kingdom and his righteousness …' (Matt. 6:33): Jesus
puts 'the establishing of God's kingdom' before our petitions in 'Your

kingdom come'. It is 'the reign of God, His sovereignty, for which we are to pray', the kingdom vision so needed by the Church. Already existing in heaven, and in hearts surrendered to Christ, Jesus calls us to pray God's kingdom power over the entire universe, restoring the world-view to health and security. When *we* lift the weapon of prayer, Satan's kingdom *must* fall.

'Your will be done on earth as it is in heaven': Scripture tells us that the angels obey God 'unquestioningly', 'speedily' and 'completely' – this model needs to be ours. Heaven can, therefore, be described as a 'totalitarian society', without the earthly negative connotations. When we obey God totally we 'find perfect freedom', and a fulfilled, perfect and healthy life. Romans 12 says that we should offer our 'bodies as living sacrifices' (vv.1–2) – God's will must overrule our self-centredness. The whole of creation is waiting!

Provided for – body, soul and spirit

Now we come to the part of the Lord's Prayer that focuses on us – having given God His rightful place. Jesus invites us to pray: 'Give us this day our daily bread', not taking God's goodness for granted, but giving heartfelt thanks. Not asking Him for *every* need can turn to pride, 'which blocks our vision' of God and others. Once we have sought His kingdom, He promises 'in days of famine they will enjoy plenty' (Psa. 37:19). God has given us abundance; but we haven't depended on Him.

Having addressed the physical part of life, 'Forgive us our trespasses, as we forgive those who trespass against us' (AV), deals with the psychological aspects of emotions, thoughts and will – here our offences against others. It seems that our greatest problem is guilt, which weighs us down, and our need for divine forgiveness – only available through Jesus' blood. When we ask for forgiveness – *and*, importantly, forgive those who have 'trespassed against us' – we seek 'the reality that God promises' to all who ask.

Recognising our deepest spiritual need, 'deliverance and protection', Jesus says we should pray: 'And lead us not into temptation, but deliver us from the evil one'. Is this unrecognised or overwhelming temptation? But, as we look at the Lord's experience in the Garden of Gethsemane, where He prayed: 'My Father, if it is possible, may this cup be taken from me' (Matt. 26:39), we see His humanity crying out in the face of temptation. Acknowledging *our* weakness and despair when faced with the possibility of sinning, gives us access to God's power, and freedom from evil's destruction.

How to be His kingdom people

In some late manuscripts, the prayer ends with an explosion of praise of God's majesty: 'For yours is the kingdom and the power and the glory for ever. Amen'. Earthly power is destined for destruction. 2 Thessalonians 2 reads: 'then the lawless one will be revealed, whom the Lord Jesus will … destroy by the splendour of his coming' (v.8). 'The LORD reigns' now (Psa. 96:10), but remember that, astonishingly, *He* waits to reign through *us*, so that His kingdom power can be at work in our world. *Pray in* the kingdom!

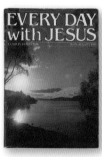

Every Day with Jesus
July/August 1983

Quotes

Jesus ... drives the mists and misconceptions from around the Deity, and shows us that the heart that throbs at the back of the universe is like His heart – a heart overflowing with unconditional love.

God offers us infinite resources for the asking and the taking – Himself. The first moments of prayer should, therefore, be contemplative, reflective, meditative. As we gaze upon God and His infinite resources, we take, as someone put it, 'a time exposure to God'. His adequacy and sufficiency are printed indelibly upon us. No matter, then, what difficulties and problems face us – we are more than a match for them. The vision of His greatness puts the whole of life in its proper perspective. 'We kneel, how weak – we rise, how full of power.'

Quotes

The greatest contribution we can make individually to the world at this present time is to demonstrate, by our lives, that the King of heaven is reigning in us. High-principled, sacrificial and serviceable living is an irrefutable argument for the fact of God's rulership in the world.

Prayer is not something by which we inform God of our needs, and thus influence Him to give things to us. Prayer is designed to influence us – it is we who are in need of this kind of prayer, not God. Of course God knows what we are in need of, but He also knows that unless we come face to face daily with the fact that we are creatures of need, then we can soon develop a spirit of independence, and withdraw ourselves from close contact and fellowship with Him. Prayer, then, is something we need.

... when we give God His rightful place, He gives us our rightful place.

Reflection

The Lord's Prayer has been said to consist of two parts: *realignment* and *result*. In the first part we realign ourselves to our Father, to His name, to His kingdom, to His will, and in the second we get the results – He gives to us, forgives us, leads us, and delivers us. These are the alternate beats of the heart of prayer. The more we realign our purposes to God's purposes the better the results. Perhaps we ought to put more emphasis on the realignment and let the results take care of themselves. If we look only at the results we are focusing on the wrong things. 'We have only one responsibility,' said Dr E. Stanley Jones, 'to live in union with God'. When we learn and practise the first part of the Lord's Prayer, the second part will take care of itself.

Prayer

Lord Jesus Christ, how wise and wonderful You are. When You were here on earth You always put first things first and the results always came out right. Help me approach life in the same way. I ask this in and through Your peerless and precious name. Amen.

The Divine
Gardener

'This is to my Father's glory, that you
bear much fruit, showing yourselves
to be my disciples'

JOHN 15:8

Quiet Time

We so often ask God
for joy
then are shocked when we
reap misery.
God plants joy eagerly
yet it sprouts
only
in the rich soil of trust
and thrives on the waters of
obedience and praise.
And it IS true that
the tender seedling of
God's joy
and the weed of
self-pity
cannot survive in the same garden!

Taken from *No Rain, No Gain* by Susan Lenzkes. Copyright ©
1995 by Susan Lenzkes and used by permission of Discovery
House Publishers, Box 3566, Grand Rapids MI 49501. All rights
reserved.

J OHN 15 TELLS US GOD CUTS OFF EVERY UNFRUITFUL branch and 'prunes those branches that bear fruit for even larger crops' (v.2, TLB): our 'spiritual fruitfulness' depends on His 'careful and relentless pruning'. Hard-sounding words, maybe, but remember it's our Father who holds the shears, who 'showed his great love for us' by making us 'alive with Christ' (Eph. 2:6). Make sure you *know* the Gardener, the true God of the Bible, shown to us through Jesus; you can trust Him with your life.

The cleansing power of His Word and presence

We read: 'For the word of God is living and active. Sharper than any double-edged sword' (Heb. 4:12); God uses His Word to make us more effective disciples. We need to continually meditate on this spiritual food and drink, or God may use other, more painful ways of getting our attention! All His comfort and counsel are in Scripture, and it cleanses: Jesus, *the* Word, 'cleansed' – spoke the truth about – the Father, His kingdom, prayer and religion.

God also prunes through the Holy Spirit, who helps us 'in times of need'; where the enemy whispers to us that sin doesn't really matter, He convicts us of its deadliness, so we can repent and ask for forgiveness. Not allowing us to rationalise our sin, or dismiss it as 'old-fashioned', He shows us its true ugliness. The enemy may tempt us to think 'everybody sins', but, because God won't let us be tempted beyond what we can bear (1 Cor. 10:13), we have power to withstand. Thank God for the Holy Spirit!

Another 'pruning knife' the Divine Gardener uses is prayer. As we pray, everything unfruitful in us can be cut away as we listen to Him. Just looking into the face of Jesus makes us *want* to be clean. In God's presence, the focus is on His will alone, so that 'we achieve His highest purposes'. We will find, too, that spending time with Him helps us work – and, therefore, rest – more effectively. Prayer also removes our desire to people-please; we live for God, and He teaches us to use time wisely and well.

Being obedient to God in the Church and the world

Our Father uses the Church to prune us. He can speak straight to our hearts through 'teaching and preaching'; small groups of 'loving, caring believers' allow correction to be received and given in love, deep needs to be shared: 'Since God so loved us, we also ought to love one another' (1 John 4:11). Personal counselling and exercising our gifts strengthens the Church; wise biblical discipline not only strengthens, but saves souls – and, most importantly, Communion shows us God's love so powerfully that it can change us to be like Him.

Romans 13 says: 'Everyone must submit himself to the governing authorities, for there is no authority except that which God has established' (v.1). God uses authority to bring peace and harmony, allowing pressures to teach and correct, where Satan brings in rebellion. Our attitude to authority – ordained by God and crucial to 'our spiritual growth and development' – shows our respect for Him. Our obedient spirits show Christlikeness, giving us the moral authority to refrain from anything ungodly.

Turning difficulties into God-opportunities

God also uses Satan's attacks to prune us, for our benefit and His glory. Jesus said: 'the prince of this world is coming. He has no hold on me' (John 14:30), and was able to turn the enemy's attacks to advantage. With Jesus controlling our lives, we can do the same. His unfailing grace prevents our defeat; in this way God amazingly ensures that Satan's harassment strengthens our faith, serving the Father's divine purposes, enabling us to grow spiritually, dependent on Him. Keep close to the Lord, and His victory is ours.

'And we know that in all things God works for the good of those who love him' (Rom. 8:28): God prunes us even in the hardest situations, using them to make us more fruitful. Even pain from difficult events, *with our co-operation*, can be used to 'smooth out the rough edges' in our souls. 'Absolute confidence and trust' in our God assures us that whatever happens is transformed through Him – in His hands hurts can make us 'better', not 'bitter'.

Lastly, our Father uses times of deprivation and loss to improve our effectiveness: in His grace He may arrange 'for us to fail in a secondary thing that we might succeed in a primary thing'. He may use difficult financial circumstances to get our attention, give us a time of 'enforced inactivity' so we can listen to Him or remove something upon which we have been depending too much.

Will *you* allow the Divine Gardener to prune you? If you do, His reward will be your fruitfulness for Him!

Every Day with Jesus
September/October 1983

Quotes

> Patience, true patience, like gold, is developed in the furnace of affliction.

Those of you ... who are struggling with some strong and fierce temptations – take heart. God is permitting you to be engaged in a battle with Satan which will not deprive you but deepen you. In His strength and power, you will emerge from this conflict with a refinement and a poise that you never thought possible. The battle will serve to show you that it is '"Not by might, nor by power, but by my Spirit," says the LORD Almighty' (Zech. 4:6). You will rejoice, not in what you can do, but in what He can do within you.

> When we get down before God in prayer, and take time to *listen* to what He has to say to us, He brings the important to the centre of consciousness and pushes the unimportant to the edge. Therefore, in ... *listening* prayer, God prunes our purposes and our persons.

Quotes

When He prunes … He will not permit anything to happen to us unless it accords with the purposes which He planned for us before the world began. So be open to Him in the days that lie ahead, for He needs your consent and co-operation if He is to do a perfect and complete job. Let Him prune you from mistakes to mastery, from despair to delight and from blunders to beauty. And when the pruning process feels painful, remember that the knife is in good and reliable hands. Your Father *is the Gardener.*

One of the most freeing insights of Scripture is the fact that God is the highest authority in the universe, and works through all lesser authorities to prune our lives and develop our effectiveness.

Reflection

C.S. Lewis spoke of God's pruning process as an 'intolerable compliment', meaning that one of the greatest tributes God can pay us as human beings is to work at producing the likeness and characteristics of His Son in our lives. Such is His longing that we become like Christ, that He will not refrain from pruning us even though at times the process may hurt. But it must always be remembered that though God may hurt us He will never harm us. Someone has put that same thought in this way: 'Whilst it is always true that God loves us as we are, it is also true that He loves us too much to let us stay as we are.' How grateful we ought to be that we are loved by a God who is committed to transforming us day by day into the image of His Son.

Prayer

O Father, I am indeed grateful. Help me surrender to Your loving hands knowing that only that which works for my highest good shall come to me. My life is Yours to do with as You will. In Jesus' name I pray. Amen.

The Vision of
God

'In the year that King Uzziah died,
I saw the Lord seated on a throne,
high and exalted, and the train of
his robe filled the temple.'

ISAIAH 6:1

Quiet Time

'Give Me of your first fruits,
that which is new and fresh,
that which you'd like to keep.'

'Does that mean I must give You,
the first hour of my day, Lord?
That hour choice for sleeping
or waking so slowly?
Do You already claim that hour
for Yourself?
Have I been robbing You?'

'You've been robbing
yourself, child!'

T O THE EXTENT THAT WE KNOW *WHO GOD IS*, WE WILL
live the way He wants. It is important to know that, through all the
increasing chaos of our world, our only security is in God, whose
kingdom and throne are unshakeable.

God's transforming presence

Even though God is far above us in His majesty, He welcomes us before
His throne of grace, where our trust and worship flow in recognition
of the work of the cross, and our anxieties vanish, for '... those who
hope in the LORD will renew their strength. They will soar on wings like
eagles ...' (Isa. 40:31).

Our Creator's transcendence and the truth of His immanence – His
presence within us – reignite our feelings of reverence and awe and
our struggles are put in their right perspective. As we pray, meditate on
and read God's Word we will come to know *the* Word, our Lord Jesus
Christ.

Psalm 46 reads: 'Be still, and know that I am God ...' (v.10). It is only
when alone with God that our picture of Him grows in truth and reality,
otherwise we can demean Him, trying to make Him more like us. When
we see God's glory, and consider how much *we* have hurt *Him* rather
than how others have hurt us, our world-view changes. Abraham said:
'Will not the Judge of all the earth do right?' (Gen. 18:25). Instead of
looking to others, shouldn't we look to our God for justice, for anything
else distorts our view? Turning towards the living God, Job's 'rebellion
dissolved and he was delivered from all his problems'. He declared, 'My
ears had heard of you but now my eyes have seen you' (Job 42:5).

Worshipping our all-sufficient and holy God

Isaiah also saw God 'was all in all' in His glory, when he proclaimed:

'... the train of his robe filled the temple' (Isa. 6:1). But we need to ask: *is He sufficient in our hearts?* Again, knowing that God is infinitely more than capable of bringing us through the worst comforts us. The need for God *and* something else (eg good health or money), means 'we do not really know God. We simply know about Him'.

In moving closer to God we risk 'all that is unlike Him being consumed and destroyed', but in this place of closeness, urgency and passion enable us to submit to Him. Knowing God's 'worth-ship', we discover our highest function is to worship the King, that 'all service is worship, and all worship is service', one flowing out of the other. Our whole being then opens to worship, praise and thanksgiving for who God is and what He does. Why worship God? C.S. Lewis wrote: 'In commanding us to worship Him, God is inviting us to enjoy Him'. Martin Luther's 'joyful exchange' then takes place – at God's invitation.

The consuming fire of God's holiness is His 'innermost reality', His name is described in Scripture as 'holy' more often than any other way. Knowing His holiness we become more aware of our sinfulness, and that God is to be honoured. The desire then deepens to obey His command: 'Be holy because I, the LORD your God, am holy' (Lev. 19:2). We desire to honour Him, showing the world that holiness brings health, where sin and evil bring death.

The cross, His grace and our obedience

Not even our unworthiness prevents our drawing close: divine grace helps us face our sin, the sin that made Isaiah cry: 'Woe to me! ... I am ruined! For I am a man of unclean lips ... and my eyes have seen the ... LORD Almighty' (Isa. 6:5). For, facing our sin, we open ourselves to God's grace, which cleanses and sustains us. We need to want to draw near. When we do draw near, His presence changes us – we then need to remember what it cost Him: His only Son.

How amazing that God *chooses* us to fulfil His purposes! Isaiah was asked: '… who will go for us?' The vision *he* had of God was enough for him to say immediately: 'Here I am. Send me!' (Isa. 6:8). Our challenge is to obey, regardless of the cost, once we have heard God's call. To be able to do that we need to 'know God well enough'.

The gospel is life – but can be death to those who refuse it. As we look at our world we see there is an urgency in obeying God's call. Out of seeing God as He really is – reigning on the eternal throne – and seeing ourselves – sinners saved by grace – comes the courage and power to step out and serve others in holiness, knowing that all our insufficiency is taken up by His *all*-sufficiency.

Every Day with Jesus
January/February 1992

> ... life works better when we know how to glance at things but *gaze* at God.

Though God reigns from a majestic throne, He is accessible to us at all times of day and night ... When a man or woman, boy or girl says, 'God be merciful to me a sinner', the message goes straight through to the throne and they receive this personal reply: 'You are forgiven, redeemed, and set free from your sin.'

The throne of God, you see, is not only a throne of righteousness but a throne of grace! Righteousness says, 'Stay back until you are good enough to approach.' Grace says, 'I will put on you the robes of righteousness that are provided for you by Christ – now you are good enough.'

Quotes

The real trouble is not that people do not have enough 'things', but that the 'things' in themselves are not enough. The plain fact is that there is ultimately only one way in which the human heart can have enough, or to be more exact, one Being that is enough for men and women, and that is God! ... Drop your anchor into the depths of this reassuring and encouraging revelation – God is the Enough. Only He is sufficient for us; only He can truly satisfy our souls. He, and only He, is enough.

I tell you, with all the conviction of my heart, that unless we are gripped by the belief that God acts justly in everything – *everything* – then we will not have the sure-footedness we need to negotiate the rocky slopes that are up ahead.

This is why a revelation of God's holiness is so important. It helps us stop pretending and start facing how bad we really are, causes us to confess that what we need only God can provide, and opens us up to tasting and appropriating divine grace in the way we ought.

Reflection

It has been said that we will never rise higher in our Christian life than our concept and vision of God. There is hardly a problem in the Christian life that cannot be traced back to a faulty vision of the Almighty. Idolatry is bowing down to a false god rather than the true God, a caricature rather than the reality. Is it possible that there can be 'Christian idolators' who carry in their hearts a false image of God drawn from the raw material of their childhood fears and guilts rather than from the true revelation which God gives us in His Word? There is no excuse for any Christian failing to see God as He really is. All we need to do is to draw lines from Jesus into infinity and there we have a perfect picture of Him. God is like Jesus for Jesus is God in human form.

Prayer

O God my Father, help me banish from my soul any caricatures or misconceptions I may have of You and develop within me a true vision of You – a God who is like Jesus. In His peerless and wonderful name I pray. Amen.

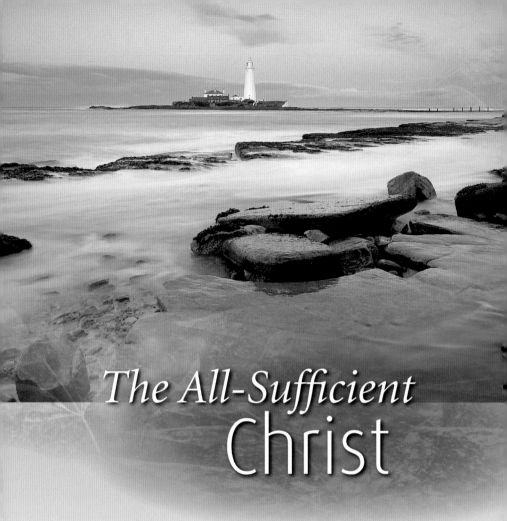

The All-Sufficient
Christ

'He is before all things, and in
him all things hold together.'
COLOSSIANS 1:17

Quiet Time

Lord, on my list of things to do,
I'm wise when I begin with You
But who comes next, and what is best?
So many needs, no time to rest!
Then when I see my list at night,
things are crossed off, but is it right?

My child, when there's so much to do,
You'll find Me waiting deep in you.
Now take those tasks from off that list –
Wrap them 'round us, so nothing's missed.
First place upon a list seems right?
When I'm your *Centre* we'll win this fight!

Susan Lenzkes, copyright © 1997

I N COLOSSIANS, PAUL WRITES TO THE CHURCHES AT Colosse (and Laodicea) to reaffirm Christ's glorious all-sufficiency. Although writing from prison, Paul's greetings overflow with words of grace and peace, encouraging them and thanking God for their faith and love springing 'from the hope that is stored up' for them in heaven (Col. 1:5).

'All over the world this gospel is bearing fruit and growing ...' (v.6): Paul reminds the believers of the 'absolute and universal' truth of the gospel, desiring that God fill them 'with the knowledge of his will through all spiritual wisdom and understanding' (v.9), to be more fruitful, 'strengthened with all power' (v.11). He reminds them – and us – they are heirs of God and joint heirs with Christ, rescued, redeemed, forgiven.

The supremacy of Christ and the servant heart

'He is the image of the invisible God, the firstborn over all creation' (v.15): Paul reminds the Church of Christ's 'supremacy and sufficiency'. Grasping this truth, we are protected from error; by His love and power 'all things hold together' (v.17), in 'perfect unity'. He is 'the head of the body, the church' (v.19); we must stay close to Him – or lose direction. In the sinless Christ is all the fullness of God (v.19); *His* gospel keeps us in the faith.

Paul reveals the suffering servant heart needed to 'present ... the word of God in its fulness' (v.25) – making Christ 'fully known' through Scripture – and making mature disciples. Christ within us, 'the hope of glory' (v.27), empowers us to correct and teach, as we 'labour' with all our energy (v.29).

Victory in Christ

Paul's longing is that the churches are 'encouraged in heart and united in love' (Col. 2:2), with unity of mind concerning the 'truths of the Bible and the supremacy of Christ' – our protection against error. All truths are ours in Christ; our journey with Him one of continuous, glorious revelation. Knowing Christ holds all wisdom and knowledge; 'fine-sounding arguments' (v.4) cannot deceive us and, as we receive from Him and surrender to Him, we are constantly empowered, growing in maturity.

Paul clearly exposes the false teaching of those like the Gnostics, who based their reasoning on human theories, believing also that matter is evil. But *Christ* took on human flesh and we 'have been given fulness [of life] in Christ' (v.10), and share our Saviour's victory. Already purified and freed by Christ, our baptism is complete – only because *He* 'cancelled the written code' (v.14) is it 'possible not to sin'. The enemy's defeat is made public at the cross. Away from the Head, Christ, we will drift away from each other, the world's rules only bring us back into bondage.

Allowing Christ to rule in our relationships

As Christians we live on earth – but also in heaven, being 'raised with Christ' (Col. 3:1). Our relationship with Him is where our focus should be, for it 'shapes every other relationship'. Paul tells us that, when Christ comes again, we will also 'appear with him in glory' (v.4) – what a relationship! But, necessarily, everything of our 'earthly nature' must be 'put to death' (v.5), if Christ's life is to flow through us; otherwise we risk God's judgment.

'Here there is no Greek or Jew … Christ is all, and is in all' (v.11): Paul deepens and widens our life in Christ and our Christian relationships. Indeed, he describes the Church as 'God's chosen people' (v.12), who should treat each other as Christ has treated them, covering everything in love that 'binds them all together in perfect unity' (v.14), bringing peace. We are to let His Word 'dwell richly' in us (v.16), ruling our churches. *Everything* is to be done in His name.

Paul then takes up the theme of family and work relationships, with surrender to God first. For the wife the word is submit ('defer in everything that is right'), for the husband it's to love (in word *and* deed) and understand, and for children it's to obey. Godly order follows godly love. Harshness, say of fathers towards children, bears bitter fruit and crushes the spirit. Christian slaves – or us in our work relationships – should obey their masters 'with sincerity of heart and reverence for the Lord' (v.22). Masters should be 'right and fair' to their slaves. Then Paul thoughtfully turns to those outside the Church: fervent prayer and praise, words spoken in love – these will bring others to Christ.

Paul's closing words are 'Remember my chains. Grace be with you' (v.18); even under severe pressure he's able to reach out and give to others. It remains to ask: 'We are all in all to Christ. But is He all in all to us?' He certainly was to Paul.

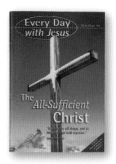

Every Day with Jesus
March/April 1998

Quotes

... in Him is found all spiritual reality. Those who depend on rituals and ceremonies for their salvation are living in the shadows. Christ is all that is needed. All.

When we continue to give ourselves to Him then we are rooted in Him, built up in Him, and our lives overflow with thankfulness. These may be mixed metaphors but they are telling nevertheless. Rooted in Christ we grow in Him. We hardly bury a seed to see the last of it. Established in Him we are built up in Him. And the final test is how thankful you are. If you do not give thanks regularly for the fact that you are favoured of God then you ought to question whether you are indeed a Christian.

God can do nothing greater for us than He has done in Christ.

Quotes

Everybody *in the Lord* is in service for the Lord. It means being involved in the Lord's plans for us. Let no unimportant weeds choke the fine wheat of the kingdom. Say 'No' to the marginal so that you can say 'Yes' to the central.

... the union that exists between Christ and His people is hidden from the eyes of the men and women of this world. Though they see us going about our tasks they are unaware that the strength by which we live and the power by which we practise our faith is drawn from another world. But believers can only enjoy and draw upon this life as they daily reach up through the avenue of prayer and avail themselves of the resources that are hidden with Christ in God.

Reflection

There are some professing Christians who are not convinced that Jesus Christ is sufficient to assure us of salvation and they claim without adding to Him other things, such as religious rituals and ceremonies, we cannot be sure of a home in heaven. The Galatian churches, you will remember, had fallen into that trap. The writer C.S. Lewis described this way of thinking as 'Christ AND ...'. Christ AND religious formalities. Christ AND legalistic observances. Religious rituals and ceremonies may be all right in their place, but we do not depend on them for salvation; it is on Christ and Christ alone. The various ceremonies of the Church may help to validate our spiritual experiences, but we must never lose sight of the fact that our faith and basis for eternal salvation lies not in what we do but in what He has done. Let nothing move you from that great fact. Nothing.

Prayer

Heavenly Father, may my confidence and hope for eternal salvation rest in the fact that You are an all-sufficient Saviour. Nothing I can do can add to that fact. My trust is in You – and in You alone. Amen.

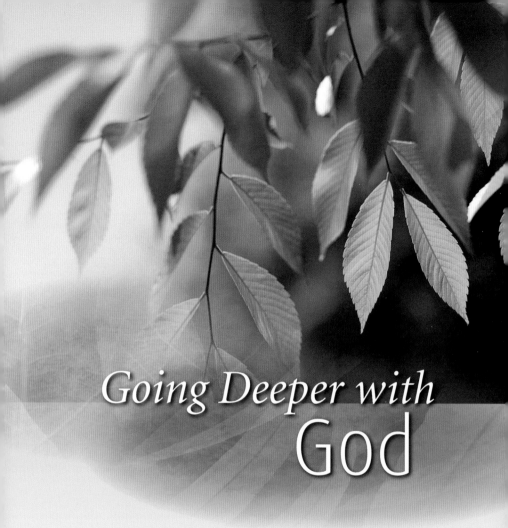

Going Deeper with God

'Therefore let us leave the
elementary teachings about
Christ and go on to maturity ...'
HEBREWS 6:1

Quiet Time

Dear child of God,
when clouds descend,
when depression wraps its
heavy cloak about your soul,
when God seems distant and
you, so alone –
stretch out a finger of faith,
for you may be closer than you've
ever been ...
He may be hiding you in the
shadow of His wing.
Beneath God's wing
deep shadow blocks our sight
and bids us hear our
darkest feelings whisper
their pain, loss, and unmet needs
into the sufficiency of God's love.

DO WE WANT TO MOVE CLOSER TO GOD? IF WE DO, AND want to 'grow in the grace and knowledge of our Lord and Saviour Jesus Christ' (2 Pet. 3:18), all our self-centredness must be put at the feet of Christ. He must be Lord of our lives; our wills 'have to capitulate to God's will' in surrender and deep repentance. This may be difficult, but the result of 'radical' repentance is the start of a deep relationship with the Almighty – 'Godly sorrow brings repentance that leads to salvation and leaves no regret' (2 Cor. 7:10). In complete surrender, we will be able to maintain a daily attitude of repentance, needed to combat our tendency to sin.

Next we consider *'how to avail ourselves of God's grace'*, for His undeserved mercy, and its accompanying power, must be received to be effective: 'how much more will those who receive God's abundant provision of grace … reign in life' (Rom. 5:17). Those who know God deeply seem to know humbly 'that there is grace to be had' – and we're all invited to 'approach the throne of grace with confidence' (Heb. 4:16). Here we will find the 'treasure' that shows us 'the values of earth in the light of heaven', and we can live in God's strength. *Receive* – God gives us more, and *always enough*.

Alone with our trustworthy God

'To go deeper with God is *to spend time with Him*': reading His Word, praying and listening for His voice – there is no substitute for our personal Quiet Time with Him, under the Holy Spirit's direction. Psalm 34 reads 'I sought the LORD, and he answered me …' (v.4): these are times to 'know Him and be known by Him' – when we seek, we will *really* find (Luke 11:9), and He will give us the resources we need. As we obey His command to 'Be still, and know that I am God …' (Psa. 46:10), He will feed our spirits.

Now we must ask if *'we have confidence in His character'*, if we doubt His goodness; if we don't trust God, we won't want closeness. When we have a deep and intimate relationship with God, we 'may feel downcast but not destroyed'. Lack of trust brings distance, made greater if we won't accept that 'life is tragic rather than orderly' this side of heaven. Instead, we must face this, and our feelings; then we can listen to God. When Job did that, God *'gave Himself'*, and he was able to say: 'My ears had heard of you but now my eyes have seen you' (Job 42:5). We can say this too, as we look at the cross.

Knowing how to *worship* God seems the hallmark of those 'who know God intimately'. And knowing God intimately leads us naturally into serving Him: when Isaiah heard God ask 'Whom shall I send?', he answered, 'Here I am. Send me!' (Isa. 6:8). Unless we are in loving relationship with Jesus, we've 'nothing of eternal value to offer to a needy world'. Worshipping Him in the midst of difficulties, drawing near 'with a sincere heart in full assurance of faith' (Heb. 10:22), we 'complete ourselves', and prepare ourselves for heaven.

Being thirsty for more

'Pursuing Him with passion' we indentify with the psalmist's cry: 'O God, you are my God, earnestly I seek you; my soul thirsts for you, my body longs for you …' (Psa. 63:1). This passion is what drives us to know God more deeply – and causes us to want even more of Him. Paul pleads: 'I want to know Christ and the power of his resurrection' (Phil. 3:10). Is there this longing in you? One main reason for our lack of thirst is our stubborn commitment to independence; a life of trust, and complete dependence on God, the best remedy.

Freedom in forgiveness and obedience

'But if you do not forgive men their sins, your Father will not forgive your sins' (Matt. 6:15): *'Christian forgiveness'* is another challenging key to a deeper relationship with God. Any refusal to forgive others *completely* as Christ has forgiven us shuts us off from Him, puts our own forgiveness in jeopardy, and denies us the freedom and release forgiveness brings. Christian forgiveness is a matter of the will, being obedient to our Lord, treating others as *He* treats us.

Next we come to the 'necessity of *obedience'*. Sadly, continued disobedience means our fellowship with God is cut off. The psalmist says: 'The law of the LORD is perfect, reviving the soul' (Psa. 19:7). As Christians we must not attempt to rationalise any 'moral or ethical issues' – 'we cannot break the commands of God; we simply break ourselves upon them'. *But,* blessings follow 'those who hear the word of God and obey it' (Luke 11:28). Indeed, commitment to Him in *all* these areas will bring unimaginably rich blessings.

Every Day with Jesus
January/February 1995

I have no hesitation in saying that if we do not understand what is involved in living repentant lives then regardless of how we start the Christian life there will be no successful continuance.

In order for our lives to work the way God designed them, the ego must be marginal and not central. In other words, Christ must be central, and the ego revolve around Him just as the planets revolve around the sun. This is quite a radical thought for any mind to grapple with, but be sure of this – if there is no acceptance of it, no change of mind on this issue, the soul will not go on to experience a deep and developing relationship with God. No change of mind about where life is to be found – no spiritual progress. It is as simple as that.

Quotes

God's great aim is not simply to bring us
into the Christian life but to develop us in it.
He is not content with calling us 'saints' but
making us saints; not simply cancelling sin
but breaking its power over us.

The Quiet Time is where the soul grows receptive, where prayer
becomes as a poet put it 'the organ of spiritual touch', where peace
flows into our turbulence, where love absorbs our resentments,
where joy heals our griefs, and where we enter into the process of
being known. The Quiet Time shuts us in with God, the door closes
upon us, and then infinite resources flood into our soul. The door
opens and we move out, with an increased awareness of God, ready
to face a world that knows so little about Him.

To know God, really know Him,
is to be made more thirsty still.

Reflection

The prophet Ezekiel saw in a vision a stream flowing from the throne of God which at first was ankle deep then later the waters became knee deep until eventually the waters became deep enough to swim in (Ezek. 47). Some Christians are content to simply paddle in the waters of God's Spirit, others are content to press in more deeply until the waters come up to their knees. Others delight themselves in God to such a degree that they find themselves in waters deep enough for them to swim. What is it like with you? Have you reached a place in your Christian life where you think that this is all there is. Be assured of this – *there's more*. Every moment we are on this earth there is more to know and experience of God than our imagination is able to conceive. Do not rest until you find waters deep enough to swim in.

Prayer

My Father and my God, forgive me if I am holding back from knowing You more deeply. Help me abandon myself to You and break with all hesitancy and cautiousness. Take me deeper into You. In Jesus' name. Amen.

Thy Will be
Done

'Do not conform any longer to the pattern
of this world, but be transformed by the
renewing of your mind. Then you will be
able to test and approve what God's will is
– his good, pleasing and perfect will.'
ROMANS 12:2

Quiet Time

Lord, You have never heard me pray,
'My will be done.'
Yet every time I fail to say,
'Thy will be done,'
You hear my silent stubborn cry
and leave me to some dead-end try.
Oh kind and patient Loving One,
I'm wiser now, 'Thy will be done!'

'**Y**OUR WILL BE DONE ON EARTH AS IT IS IN HEAVEN' (Matt. 6:10): how can we discover, and become better 'receivers' of, God's guidance and will? Scripture gives clear guidelines but, firstly, we need confidence in God's 'good, pleasing and perfect will' (Rom. 12:2), refusing Satan's lies.

Believing in the goodness of God and His guidance

We need a 'willing spirit' (Psa. 51:12), not a rebellious one that separates us from God, one that, with His grace, rejoices despite difficulties. Paul says: '… I rejoice in what was suffered for you' (Col. 1:24): the rewards are those of eternal glory, learning 'the secrets of the Lord', knowing difficulties can develop the fruit of the Spirit in us, and help us comfort others. Holding grudges against God only 'dams the stream' of His grace.

We also need assurance that God *wants* to guide us: 'I will instruct you and teach you in the way you should go …' (Psa. 32:8). Knowing that '… those who are led by the Spirit of God are sons of God' (Rom. 8:14), emphasises the importance of Almighty God leading us, not circumstances, or the lies of horoscopes. God guides us – His heirs, and co-heirs with Christ – as He guided the people of Scripture, and has led His people down the ages. Our trustworthy God guides even non-believers, and, looking back often reveals He led us unawares, 'bringing to pass His perfect purposes'.

Prayer and obedience to the Word

Often we need 'to know God's will prior to an event'. Prayer is the first thing we should turn to. Through 'uninterrupted communication' and an intimate relationship with our Lord, we learn His will and how eager He is to guide us. We will be better equipped as 'Christ's ambassadors'

(2 Cor. 5:20), able to receive wisdom because of increased sensitivity to His voice, and learn from Scripture, knowing that: 'The eyes of the Lord are on the righteous and his ears are attentive to their cry …' (Psa. 34:15).

Reading the Bible also draws us closer to God: 'If you hold to my teaching, you are really my disciples. Then you will know the truth …' (John 8:31–32). Studying the Scriptures closely, hearing, believing and obediently practising the truth, brings full understanding. We should not twist Scripture's meaning, or use it to support every decision, but submit to the Holy Spirit's guiding as we read, because 'The unfolding of your words gives light …' (Psa. 119:130). Most of our questions are answered in God's 'revealed will', the Bible.

Making Him Lord in our lives

God's main concern is 'not service but character'. He looks for our willingness to be like Christ, leading Spirit-filled lives. Surrendering to God to allow His character to grow in us enables us to hear His voice, His personal will or plan for our lives. God leaves us to make many decisions, but directs us in making 'wise spiritual decisions', sometimes through means other than the Bible. He says: 'I guide you in the way of wisdom and lead you along straight paths' (Prov. 4:11) – never contradicting His Word, guiding us to His ends, not our own. As we are '… still before the Lord', waiting 'patiently for him …' (Psa. 37:7) as a daily discipline, the closer we'll be to Him and the clearer will be our understanding of His ways.

Learning how God can guide

God uses Scripture, and its principles, to help us on personal issues, 'For everything that was written in the past was written to teach us …' (Rom. 15:4). He uses the Holy Spirit's witness in our hearts; again, the more time we spend expectantly with Him, the clearer the 'quiet witness of the Spirit' will be.

The fellowship of small groups also provides counsel and 'prayerful objectivity': 'Dear friends, let us love one another, for love comes from God' (1 John 4:7). Sometimes our personal desires are in line with God's plans for us, and He may confirm these through someone who knows us well.

God also guides through circumstances, sometimes 'quickening our imagination' or creating 'a concern' in our heart, and through inviting us to reason with Him – in 'the light of God'. He still uses supernatural means, too – dreams, visions and angels: 'All these are the work of one and the same Spirit, and he gives them to each one, just as he determines' (1 Cor. 12:11).

So, submitting our will to God, coming before Him in listening prayer and reading Scripture are all important as we seek guidance. Reasoning with God, not hurrying our decisions, talking to a mature Christian friend and reviewing our circumstances can then follow; but sometimes a step of faith is still needed. How comforting that God is willing to share our burden of making responsible decisions, and that 'the Almighty takes a personal interest in the affairs' of each one of us!

Every Day with Jesus
September/October 2000

Unquestionably God guides.
Begin by accepting the fact,
pursue it with humility and
patience, take an interest in
the experiences of others,
and you too can say: 'God
led me all the way.'

Unless we have confidence in the fact that God has
our best interests at heart then we are neither going
to seek His will nor agree to it if it is revealed. Before
you get down on your knees and ask God to show
you His will, then, it is vital that you make sure your
concept of God is in harmony with Scripture. In
other words, you must believe He is good and desires
what is best for us.

  One of the most serious obstacles on the road to
knowing God's will is the suspicion that it may not
be beneficial for us.

Quotes

... before we can know God's mind we must give Him our minds.

How, then, do we make ourselves ready to receive God's will? The first thing that is required of us, of course, is that we pray. As I look back on my life I am convinced that if prayer had had a larger place in my daily activities then God's way would have been more clear in times of perplexity, I would have been more receptive to His voice, and the Bible would have spoken with greater power. Where there is poverty in prayer there will be perplexity in the mind.

I have no hesitation in saying that the voice of God and the direction of the Holy Spirit are likely to come through most easily and most clearly to those whose minds have been tuned into the divine wavelength by the reading and study of the Scriptures.

Reflection

Professor Henry Drummond once said that there are two classes of Christians in the world – 'those who have God's will in their character and those who have God's will in their career'. Those who belong to the first class live out their lives in correspondence with the ethical principles of the Christian faith but they miss the secret whisperings of God in the ear, the constant message from heaven to earth that helps guide their feet along life's road. Never believe that the affairs of your life are too trivial for God to take notice. The God who guides the spinning stars in space notices the needs of His children on this microscopic earth. He condescends to listen to our prayers and guide us in our daily decision-making. Rejoice in the fact as did king David: 'You guide me with your counsel, and afterwards you will take me into glory' (Psa. 73:24).

Prayer

Heavenly Father, though many things about guidance are not clear to me, help me lay hold of the fact that nothing is too trivial for omniscience. Make Your will clear and plain to me I pray. In Jesus' name. Amen.

The Care of the
Soul

'... train yourself to be godly.'
1 TIMOTHY 4:7

Quiet Time

Lord, what have I gained
if I eat wisely and well
but neglect to dine at Your table;
if I work out faithfully
while failing to exercise love;
if I give myself to the
pursuit of fitness
yet am not fit for Your kingdom?
Earthly disciplines fortify
the body for a lifetime.
Heavenly disciplines strengthen
the soul for an eternity.

Susan Lenzkes, copyright © 1996

P AUL TELLS TIMOTHY: '... TRAIN YOURSELF TO BE godly' (1 Tim. 4:7) – so 'prepare for a workout'! This exercise programme, however, relying on 'spiritual experiences' *and* 'disciplined effort', is solely credited to 'the grace of God' (1 Cor. 15:10). Liberty not legalism is found in being disciplined *in Christ*, and makes us more like Him, as we receive His grace.

In God's presence with the Word, prayer and worship

Reading (and listening to) *God's Word* regularly – preferably daily – to exercise the soul, trains us powerfully for godliness. In 2 Timothy 3:16 we read, 'All Scripture is God-breathed and is useful for teaching, rebuking, correcting and training in righteousness ...'. We need to live 'on every word that comes from the mouth of God' (Matt. 4:4), studying it in depth, and warming 'ourselves at the fire of meditation'.

Next, *prayer* – the second most important exercise. Without prayer we stop 'breathing spiritually', which explains why the enemy will do all he can to stop us praying. God delights in talking to us; indeed Jesus' *command* is to 'always pray and not give up' (Luke 18:1). Being undisciplined, doubtful or self-sufficient are often barriers to prayer; but meditating on God's Word before we start helps us to be open as we talk and listen to Him.

The exercise of *worship*, as we 'focus the soul's attention on God', deepens our understanding of Him and His worthiness: 'You are worthy, our Lord and God, to receive glory and honour and power ...' (Rev. 4:11). One glimpse of Him, and 'in spirit and in truth' we fall down and worship Him, alive in the Spirit, strengthened by the Word: 'God is spirit and his worshippers must worship in spirit and in truth' (John 4:24).

Giving to God and giving Him away

Jesus often used the next exercise of the soul – *solitude* – for 'spiritual purposes'. After ministering physical and spiritual help to the people, He would go 'out to a solitary place' (Luke 4:42), for strength, for refreshment, to pray and listen to His Father. In the same way, we need solitude to listen for God's 'gentle whisper' (1 Kings 19:12). Giving Him ourselves, we are better able to help others.

Stewardship: we have been entrusted with God's interests and possessions, and godly use of these keep our souls well exercised. Good use of time – Jesus was never in a hurry – ensures we walk in God's purposes. Acknowledging all we have belongs to Him, and giving Him access to all of it, is a mark of our spiritual maturity, and affects how we dispose of it. And, as we use our talents for serving others, we will reflect our Lord's servant heart.

Next, the discipline of boldly *sharing our faith* with others. We're told: 'Always be prepared to give an answer to everyone ... for the hope that you have' (1 Pet. 3:15), for Jesus calls us His witnesses (Acts 1:8) and ours is a gospel of 'finding, not keeping' – to keep the Holy Spirit flowing in, we must allow Him to flow out, or the 'Christian heart ceases to beat'.

Getting down to basics

If we adopt 'the discipline of *simplicity*' we'll reflect our Lord, wonderful and powerful in His lack of complication or pretence; indeed He commanded us to 'become like little children' (Matt. 18:3) to receive the kingdom. Moreover, we're first to seek the kingdom of God (Matt. 6:33), then live and speak simply, 'slaves' only to Christ.

Fasting 'does wonders for the soul': Jesus taught and practised fasting, saying: 'When the bridegroom will be taken from them; then they will fast' (Matt. 9:15). But how many of us do fast? Motive is crucially important. The spiritual purpose of fasting is to strengthen our prayer, 'discover God's guidance', be an act of repentance – *then*, God's blessings will flow.

Confession, forgiveness and 'keeping on'

Confession and forgiveness are next. By confessing to God first, then others, we cleanse our souls of sin. Forgiveness, too, benefits the soul – if we don't forgive others 'your Father will not forgive you' (Matt. 6:15). We must forgive 'as the Lord forgave you' (Col. 3:13) – for guilt and unforgiveness lead to sick bodies and souls.

The last spiritual exercise is *perseverance*: we need to keep running 'with perseverance the race marked out for us' (Heb. 12:1). The Holy Spirit's grace gives us the self-control we need, because the godliness we are in training for 'has value for all things' (1 Tim. 4:8), not least overcoming our difficulties and problems.

'The practice of spiritual disciplines' leads us to godliness, with their focus the Lord Jesus Christ. Let's see everything through His eyes, for 'we are in training for eternity'. Paul tells us that 'godliness with contentment is great gain' (1 Tim. 6:6): are you prepared to train for the race? Then *keep running.*

Every Day with Jesus
January/February 1997

" The effective Christian life is a balanced life. Being dependent means we draw our life from Another; being disciplined means we pay attention to the ways by which we draw from that Other. Dependence plus discipline makes dependable disciples. "

Worship most certainly is 'the response of a heart in love with God', but how does the heart become filled with love for God? Though we do not develop love for God by self-effort we can focus the soul's attention on God, His attributes and character. The more we focus on God the more responsive we become to Him, and the more responsive we become to Him the more godly we become. Thus we can train ourselves to be godly by commanding our souls to stand to attention before God, to focus on Him and reflect on His love, His holiness and His glory.

" It is through discipline that we assent to God's purposes for our lives. "

Quotes

The Christian faith: to know Jesus as Saviour and Lord and to help others know Him as Saviour and Lord. These two matters constitute the heartbeats of the gospel: intake and outflow, receptivity and response. And if both the processes are not in operation the Christian heart ceases to beat.

The awful thing about sin … is not only that it breaks God's law but that it breaks His heart. We must tell Him we are sorry about that, naming the transgression so that we are clear about what we are confessing. Have no fear as to how to approach God for access to God has been made easy through Jesus. Our Lord's awful purity was not forbidding but forgiving. If you dare to expose your heart to His heart you will find not merely relief but release. And you must find that, for with guilt in your system your soul will turn sour. Then if we have wronged others we must make confession to them too. Confession must be always as wide as the circle of offence.

Reflection

Thousands of years ago King Solomon said this: 'I went past the field of the sluggard, past the vineyard of the man who lacks judgment; thorns had come up everywhere, the ground was covered with weeds, and the stone wall was in ruins. I applied my heart to what I observed and learned a lesson from what I saw' (Prov. 24:30–32). Those words could well describe the condition of someone who has neglected to cultivate his or her soul. Left to itself, without loving care and attention, the soul soon becomes like a garden overgrown with weeds. When the soul is neglected we experience all kinds of problems, obsessions, addictions, loss of meaning and emotional pain. How good are you at cultivating your soul? Always remember God created your soul for a relationship with Himself. The more we develop that relationship the more our souls will function in the way they were designed.

Prayer

Gracious and loving heavenly Father, help me as Your Word commands to train myself to be godly (1 Tim. 4:7). Whatever I neglect, let it not be the needs of my soul. In Jesus' name I pray.

The Pursuit of
Excellence

'If you have raced with men on foot
and they have worn you out, how
can you compete with horses?'
JEREMIAH 12:5

Quiet Time

Before I was born
You delivered me.
Before I knew the feel of You,
Your hand was upon me.
You said,
'See, I am setting before you
the way of life and the way of death.
Stand at the crossroads and look;
ask for the ancient paths,
ask where the good way is
and walk in it.
Obey me, and I will be your God
and you will be mine.'
So I chose to follow the good way.
And I found that I was in pursuit of
You ...
for you are the most excellent Way,
the perfect Truth,
and the only Life.

Susan Lenzkes, copyright © 1996

J EREMIAH WONDERFULLY SHOWS THE MEANING OF spiritual faithfulness as the prophet fulfils his destiny from God. He is comforted by the thought that he is known by God – 'Before I formed you in the womb I knew you' (1:5) – he's equipped by Him, *in* his inadequacy, with visions that teach: 'never underestimate God and never overestimate evil'.

Through Jeremiah, God powerfully accuses Israel of 'spiritual promiscuity': 'My people have ... forsaken me ... and have dug their own cisterns ...' (2:13) – mirroring the stubborn independence *we* so often prefer. Anger at Israel's complacency then softens to passionate pleas to repent of their hardness of heart.

Sin and its consequences

Destruction by Babylon is their judgment; but the priests try to cover up the people's sin 'as though it were not serious' (6:14), denying Scripture's truth, believing their protection was in obeying rituals. Are we guilty of this, and of allowing our relationship with God to crumble? His judgment may seem harsh but His love won't let us stay as we are.

Jeremiah shows anger towards the people's sin, but also immense compassion – knowing the devastation the invasion will bring. We too need this godly compassion for our Church and world. Then God denounces the nation's idolatry – so appealing to us, too, because it expresses 'our need to worship' without 'the necessity for inward change'. More seriously, the people had broken the 'marriage' covenant with God, so sorrowful that He refuses to 'listen when they call to me' (11:14).

A frightened Jeremiah, plagued with doubts as he learns that some want him killed, cries out: 'Why does the way of the wicked prosper?' (12:1). God's reply, as it is to us, is to trust Him; His justice *will be done*. Despite hearing that their wickedness has disqualified them from being part of God's purposes, the people remain unrepentant: Jeremiah's tears cannot persuade a heartbroken God to change His judgment.

Jeremiah is told by God not to pray, and we are given insight into his despair and hurt: 'Why is my pain unending and my wound grievous and incurable?' (15:18) – this is 'honest praying', sharing our feelings with God. However, God calls him to repent – why? Because Jeremiah was standing for the people, *against* God; however, his repentance brings God's restoration.

Obedience, such as keeping '… the Sabbath day holy …' (17:22) brings God's blessings, as does repentance. Jeremiah sees a potter shaping a new vessel from discarded clay: illustrating what God does once we repent. Hardened hearts, however, He can only break with His judgment. Beaten for speaking the truth, Jeremiah rightly brings his spiritual battle of despair and rejoicing to God.

Hope and perseverance

In the midst of darkness, God gives a glimpse of the coming Messiah: 'The days are coming … when I will raise up … a righteous Branch' (23:5), a striking contrast with the corrupt kings and false prophets of the day. At this time, the 'cream of Judah's society' are captives in Babylon; in these exiles, open to God's leading, lies the future.

After faithfully 'calling them to repent' for 23 years, Jeremiah reveals God's full judgment of 70 years of captivity in Babylon and Jerusalem's destruction. Some believe him, despite the words of false prophets. Telling the exiles to seek the Lord, he also conveys God's tender words of restoration. Hope continues to pour out as God says: '… you will be my people, and I will be your God' (30:22). And, though Jeremiah is now in prison, God continues to encourage him in words that apply to us too: 'Call to me and I will answer you …' (33:3).

King Zedekiah foolishly, and arrogantly, tries to bargain with God; but it is 'heart-change' that God always looks for – just as He calls us now to live for Him and stand 'firm on His truth'. Jeremiah is as faithful as ever to the Word of God despite further beatings, imprisonment and near death, only saved by the godly Ebed-Melech. Fighting, instead of surrendering to, the Babylonians, brings utter disaster and death for Zedekiah in Babylon.

God's will fulfilled

In contrast, Jeremiah is respected by Nebuchadnezzar, who says: '... do for him whatever he asks' (39:12). But Jeremiah chooses to return to ruined Jerusalem, trusting God. However, taken to Egypt (representing false safety) by fellow Jews fleeing the Babylonians, he faithfully continues to give God's Word, foretelling the overthrow of Egypt, and telling his countrymen that, because they disobeyed God, they will never return home. Out of God's will they sink into 'debauchery and pagan worship'; as *we* forget past lessons, we too can drift from God.

Reflecting God's missionary heart to bring all peoples to Himself, Jeremiah preaches to the nations. The oracle prophesying Babylon's destruction, reminds us that Babylon, representing pride, is destroyed – Jerusalem, representing surrender to God, still stands today. God's Word 'will always be fulfilled' and 'endures for ever'.

Every Day with Jesus
July/August 1996

Quotes

Never forget – God has feelings too. It breaks His heart to see the waywardness and obstinacy of His people. How different our lives would be if we could see that sin is not just a collision with the divine will but a wound in the divine heart.

We ought to be encouraged and humbled by the fact that though we mess up God's original purposes for our lives by our recalcitrancy and stubbornness, He nevertheless pursues His purposes with us still. It might not be what He originally wanted. But His skill and power can make something of us beyond what we dare imagine or even deserve. If by your sin or failure you have frustrated God's original purpose but have repented and come back to God, take heart. He may not be able to achieve His original purpose but He can make something beautiful of you still.

Quotes

> If we allow God's Word to so live and take root within us, when our hurts and frustrations scream within, God's Word will burn in us with His warming love, and we will hear His message above the din.

When we concentrate more on our own careers or our own future than on the purpose of God for our lives we become ego-centred rather than God-centred. That does not mean it is wrong to think and plan out a career. It means rather that unless God has first claim on our lives then we live superficially no matter how much money we make or how many possessions we own. True greatness in His kingdom is serving Him and others before ourselves (Luke 22:26–27).

> Doing the work of God faithfully is the excellence He looks for.

Reflection

There are many Old Testament prophets who demonstrate excellence in the way they carried out their God-given tasks, but Jeremiah seems to rise head and shoulders above them all. Even when the circumstances of his life led him to accuse God of tricking him and deceiving him, and his emotions screamed out in frustration and pain, the word God had given to him as a young man screamed the loudest (see Jer. 1:5; 20:9).

Spiritual excellence does not mean that we never question God or admit to doubts arising in our hearts, or even pass through what someone has described as 'the dark night of the soul'. It lies in doubting those doubts and believing our beliefs – the beliefs that we were given in the clear light of day. Spiritual excellence has many characteristics but not least is being faithful to that which God has committed to us.

Prayer

O God my Father, help me to allow Your Word to take root deep
within me so that when my emotions scream out in frustration
at what may be happening, Your Word will scream the loudest.
In Jesus' name. Amen.

The Uniqueness of our Faith

'Dear friends, although I was very eager to write to you about the salvation we share, I felt I had to write and urge you to contend for the faith that was once for all entrusted to the saints.'

JUDE 3

Quiet Time

God created our eyes –
and we looked for alternatives.
He formed our ears –
and we listened to wrong voices.
He gave us feet –
and we walked away from Him into
loss, loneliness, and despair.
So God created
a Light through the darkness –
and He is the Way.
A Promise amid lies –
and He is the Truth.
A Hope at the graveside –
and He is our Life.

J UDE COMMANDS US TO '... CONTEND FOR THE FAITH that was once for all entrusted to the saints' (v.3). In these days of multi-faith acceptance and pleas for world unity, we must clearly understand Christianity's truths. Uniquely, it claims that, apart from Jesus, 'Salvation is found in no-one else ...' (Acts 4:12). It is the only world faith claiming 'its great teacher was God incarnate', Christ's 'call is to all humanity'.

Not just a prophet, 'The Word became flesh and made his dwelling among us' (John 1:14); He *is* God's search for mankind.

Philosophy – illustrated by the attempts to will ourselves 'to do good and be good' – and moralism – the Pharisees' self-effort is an example – have both failed to find God. Christianity teaches that salvation, initiated by God, is a love-gift from Him, seen in the historical life, death and resurrection of His Son Jesus – 'the meeting point of the human and the divine'.

Jesus Christ our Saviour

Another aspect of Christian uniqueness is the 'Person of our Lord Himself'; Peter said: 'You have the words of eternal life' (John 6:68). Christ's teaching – 'as one who had authority' (Matt. 7:29) – was unparalleled because He was 'Reality itself', the sinless God Himself was speaking. Jesus called Himself 'one greater than the temple' (Matt. 12:6), accepted worship as God from His disciples (John 20:28), and claimed 'to be greater than the Scriptures'. Only He could add the commandment of 'Love one another. As I have loved you ...' (John 13:34), giving us *Someone* not something to live by. Also, Christ alone had 'authority on earth to forgive sins' (Matt. 9:6). All our worship belongs to *Him*, 'by sovereign right'.

Christianity teaches personal salvation, other religions 'self-salvation'.

Christ's death on the cross won our salvation, which often only our pride prevents our receiving. When Jesus said: 'It is finished' (John 19:30), *He* had done it all, and fasting or good works cannot save us. True conversion for Christians is passing into God's kingdom – not changing to another religion – being made 'alive with Christ' (Eph. 2:5), changed from the inside out, with a 'new life, a new relationship', faith expressing itself through love. Only Christianity gives the assurance of being saved and sanctified, for Jesus '… is able to save completely those who come to God through him …' (Heb. 7:25). *Take God at His Word.*

The written Word of God
'All Scripture is God-breathed …' (2 Tim. 3:16). Other religions have their books, but the Bible 'is unique because of its Author'. No others mention our Saviour as God's beloved Son – indeed the Qu'ran says that Allah would not 'beget a Son' – but Jesus is the Bible's 'main theme'. The true God *is* a Father – who sent His Son that we 'might have a Divine Father also'. Many authors wrote the Bible over hundreds of years, yet Christ unifies it from beginning to end. Divinely inspired, the 'word of our God stands for ever' (Isa. 40:8).

The glory of the cross, the resurrection and the ascension
The cross, 'foolishness to those who are perishing' (1 Cor. 1:18), is a stumbling-block to other religions. Our God of eternal love is merciful *because of* the cross, Christ's sacrificial spirit holding the key to its mystery. Sin and evil stand between us and God, who proclaims the cross is the only way to restore our fellowship with Him. Christ is 'the sacrifice of atonement' (Rom. 3:25). God's redemptive self-sacrifice, taking on our sin and its suffering, is unique to Christianity.

'God raised this Jesus to life, and we are all witnesses of the fact' (Acts

2:32): Christianity alone has a Founder who was resurrected, totally, not just spiritually – otherwise *there is no salvation.* Theories of fainting, being in a stupor, reincarnation or living on 'in our memories' cannot explain the disciples' powerful encounter with the risen Christ on Easter Day that never left them. When the disciples went into the open tomb, all they saw were graveclothes, lying undisturbed as though He had 'passed through' them – destroying death and bringing 'life and immortality to light' (2 Tim. 1:10). The resurrection 'assures us of God's forgiveness', of His power to change us, and His ultimate triumph over death.

'He was taken up before their very eyes …' (Acts 1:9): Christ's ascension – or exaltation – has placed Him '… above all rule and authority, power and dominion …' (Eph. 1:21). Christ has gone before us, so that we may go there too.

Remembering it is 'only Christ' for whom we can claim superiority, we should be loving towards those of other faiths, while bringing them the truth of the gospel; some 'light' can be found in other religions. From Jesus, however, 'the true light that gives light to every man' (John 1:9), flows *all* truth and beauty. He said, 'I am the way and the truth and the life. No-one comes to the Father except through me' (John 14:6).

Every Day with Jesus
March/April 1995

Quotes

"Christianity is essentially a rescue religion; it is the announcement of good news – the good news that God has come in the Person of His Son to save us from the power of sin, the penalty of sin, and one day in the future the presence of sin.

One religion as good as another? How utterly absurd. It sounds broadminded but actually it is the judgment of ignorance. No one would ever make that statement if they understood the purpose of Christ's coming to this world, His atoning death on the cross, and His glorious resurrection. We are not unmindful of the spiritual glow which comes from other lamps, but our claim for Jesus is the claim He made for Himself – He alone is the Light of the world, and thus utterly indispensable to salvation.

Quotes

The human heart longs for certainty – it needs to know without a shadow of doubt that the salvation of the soul is secure. The good news is that in Jesus Christ such security is found.

Our Lord has no peers, no rivals and no successors. He is so different from every other leader, so unique, so superior, that He qualifies for a place on His own. The things He said about God are not the same as the sayings of any other religious teacher. The claims He made for Himself ... are not ones that have been made by anyone else. His condemnation of human life and society goes deeper and is more devastating than that pronounced by any other man. The challenges and demands He made on His followers are more searching than those put forward by anyone – past and present.

The cross humbles all pride and dashes all hope of self-salvation.

Reflection

In the USA there is a poster dated 4 July 1776 in which the Declaration of Independence has been printed in such a way that the type presents a portrait of George Washington. It is possible if one is not quick on the uptake to read the text without seeing the portrait. That, however, would be an impoverishment since it was the man who made the declaration possible. To some the Bible is just literature, and they stop at the manuscripts, but we must pass through the manuscripts to the Man Christ Jesus, the supreme Being of which the book is the biography. 'Christianity' it has been said 'is Christ'. If He is withdrawn from it then the whole system crumbles and collapses. We must resist every effort to reduce Jesus to the level of a mere prophet. He is that but so much more. We are what we are because He is who He is.

Prayer

Lord Jesus Christ, help me never to stop at the pages of Scripture but advance through them into Your presence and relate to You – the Word that is bigger than human words. In Your peerless name I pray. Amen.

Stand alone editions of books featured in *Every Day with Jesus Treasury*

Every Day with Jesus Bible Classics

Although the issues of *Every Day with Jesus* from which this treasury is compiled are no longer available, you may be interested to know that four of them are available in a beautifully presented, undated format. The content of these is based on the original dated *Every Day with Jesus* which you have 'tasted' in this book.

The Lord's Prayer and *The 23rd Psalm* present two of the most encouraging and instructive passages from the Bible in a way that will inspire enquiring minds.

The Divine Gardener shows how God is at work shaping our lives and *The Divine Eagle* illustrates how God sometimes pushes us out of our comfortable world towards a deeper faith in Him.

The Divine Eagle
ISBN: 1-85345-190-8

The Divine Gardener
ISBN: 1-85345-191-6

The 23rd Psalm
ISBN: 1-85345-192-4

The Lord's Prayer
ISBN: 1-85345-193-2

£4.99 each

National Distributors

UK: (and countries not listed below)
CWR, Waverley Abbey House, Waverley Lane, Farnham, Surrey GU9 8EP.
Tel: (01252) 784700 Outside UK +44 1252 784700

AUSTRALIA: CMC Australasia, PO Box 519, Belmont, Victoria 3216.
Tel: (03) 5241 3288

CANADA: Cook Communications Ministries, PO Box 98, 55 Woodslee Avenue, Paris, Ontario.
Tel: 1800 263 2664

GHANA: Challenge Enterprises of Ghana, PO Box 5723, Accra.
Tel: (021) 222437/223249 Fax: (021) 226227

HONG KONG: Cross Communications Ltd, 1/F, 562A Nathan Road, Kowloon.
Tel: 2780 1188 Fax: 2770 6229

INDIA: Crystal Communications, 10-3-18/4/1, East Marredpalli, Secunderabad – 500026, Andhra Pradesh.
Tel/Fax: (040) 27737145

KENYA: Keswick Books and Gifts Ltd, PO Box 10242, Nairobi.
Tel: (02) 331692/226047 Fax: (02) 728557

MALAYSIA: Salvation Book Centre (M) Sdn Bhd, 23 Jalan SS 2/64, 47300 Petaling Jaya, Selangor.
Tel: (03) 78766411/78766797 Fax: (03) 78757066/78756360

NEW ZEALAND: CMC Australasia, PO Box 36015, Lower Hutt.
Tel: 0800 449 408 Fax: 0800 449 049

NIGERIA: FBFM, Helen Baugh House, 96 St Finbarr's College Road, Akoka, Lagos.
Tel: (01) 7747429/4700218/825775/827264

PHILIPPINES: OMF Literature Inc, 776 Boni Avenue, Mandaluyong City.
Tel: (02) 531 2183 Fax: (02) 531 1960

SINGAPORE: Armour Publishing Pte Ltd, Block 203A Henderson Road, 11–06 Henderson Industrial Park, Singapore 159546.
Tel: 6 276 9976 Fax: 6 276 7564

SOUTH AFRICA: Struik Christian Books, 80 MacKenzie Street, PO Box 1144, Cape Town 8000.
Tel: (021) 462 4360 Fax: (021) 461 3612

SRI LANKA: Christombu Books, 27 Hospital Street, Colombo 1.
Tel: (01) 433142/328909

TANZANIA: CLC Christian Book Centre, PO Box 1384, Mkwepu Street, Dar es Salaam.
Tel/Fax: (022) 2119439

USA: Cook Communications Ministries, PO Box 98, 55 Woodslee Avenue, Paris, Ontario, Canada.
Tel: 1800 263 2664

ZIMBABWE: Word of Life Books, Shop 4, Memorial Building, 35 S Machel Avenue, Harare.
Tel: (04) 781305 Fax: (04) 774739

For email addresses, visit the CWR website: www.cwr.org.uk
CWR is a registered charity – number 294387

Day and Residential Courses
Counselling Training
Leadership Development
Biblical Study Courses
Regional Seminars
Ministry to Women
Daily Devotionals
Books and Videos
Conference Centre

Trusted all Over the World

CWR HAS GAINED A WORLDWIDE reputation as a centre of excellence for Bible-based training and resources. From our headquarters at Waverley Abbey House, Farnham, England, we have been serving God's people for 40 years with a vision to help apply God's Word to everyday life and relationships. The daily devotional Every Day with Jesus is read by nearly a million people in more than 150 countries, and our unique courses in biblical studies and pastoral care are respected all over the world. Waverley Abbey House provides a conference centre in a unique setting.

For free brochures on our seminars and courses, conference facilities, or a catalogue of CWR resources, please contact us at the following address.
CWR, Waverley Abbey House, Waverley Lane, Farnham, Surrey GU9 8EP, UK

Telephone: **+44 (0)1252 784700**
Email: **mail@cwr.org.uk**
Website: **www.cwr.org.uk**

CRUSADE FOR WORLD REVIVAL
Applying God's Word to everyday life and relationships

Every Day with Jesus

With nearly a million readers an issue, this bestselling daily Bible reading tool offers practical help with life's challenges and insight into the deeper truths of Scripture. It is designed to challenge, inspire, comfort and encourage readers in their spiritual walk as they study six topics in depth each year.

£1.99 each issue
ISSN: 0967-1889

Annual UK subscription (6 issues)
£11.50

Also available in large print format
Single issue £1.99
Annual UK subscription £11.50

Annual daily email
£10.00

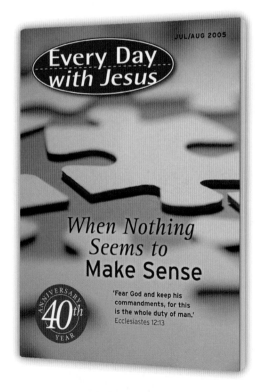

EDWJ for New Christians

A powerful and relevant guide for people new to the Christian faith or for people who need the basics presented to them clearly and dynamically. A favourite with churches across denominations.

£2.49
ISBN: 1-85345-133-9

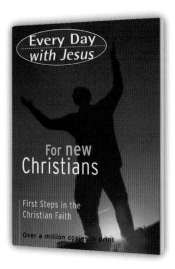

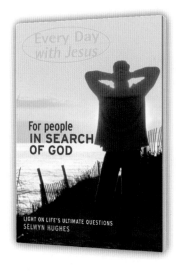

EDWJ for People in Search of God

This is a great tool for friendship evangelism, because when it comes to those hard, demanding questions people want clear, thoughtful answers. Here Selwyn Hughes offers an intelligent and helpful perspective on those big issues, including:

• What is life all about?
• Is there life after death?
• Who is God and what is He like?
• How can we know God?
• Why does God allow suffering?

£1.99
ISBN: 1-85345-226-2

Every Day with Jesus Perpetual Calendar
Time with God

CWR brings you a new calendar in this popular day-by-day flip-over desktop style. Each day has a thought and verse to encourage us to spend every day with Jesus.

£6.99
Code: EDWJPERP

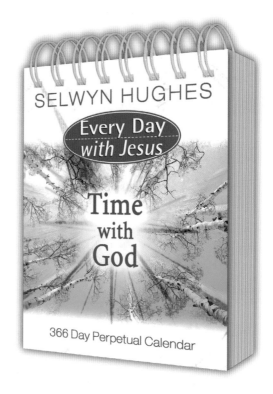

A Life Lived Every Day with Jesus

My Story

Selwyn Hughes traces his story from his roots in Wales through his conversion and call to the ministry, his experiences as a pastor to his pioneering in the fields of Christian counselling and training.

The depth of Selwyn's love and relationship with God shines through, making *My Story* both inspiring and faith building.

£9.99 (plus p&p)
ISBN: 1-85345-296-3

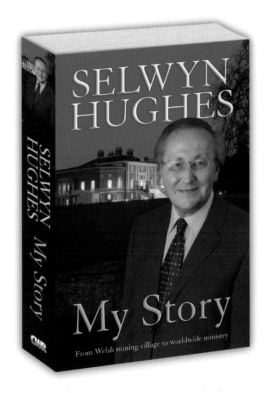